A Quiz about the
Man in Your Life

Do You Know Your Husband?

DAN CARLINSKY

sourcebooks

$\mathcal{T}$hink you know all about the man on the other side of the dinner table? Well, maybe. Let this little book be the judge.

The fact is, no matter how long you've been together, there's probably plenty you don't know about the man in your life.

Counselors say that knowing about your partner's past and preferences can be important—even things like "Who was his best friend in grade school?" and "Does he hate squash?" Knowing, they say—even knowing such bits of trivia—is a sign of caring.

So grab a pencil and show what you know. The answers, of course, are not in the book; only he can say. So after you've completed the test, ask him to check your answers and figure out your score.

The test has 100 questions. Count ten points for each correct answer. Where you miss some of a multipart question, divide and take partial credit; you'll need all the help you can get. Here's how to rate yourself:

> **Above 900:** Very impressive. In fact, downright amazing.
>
> **700–900:** Pretty good, but there's still room for improvement.
>
> **Below 700:** Weak. Ask him to give you a remedial course.

You may find you have something to brag about, or you may be humbled. Either way, just by going over your answers together, you'll learn a little and have some fun as well. Good luck.

—D.C.

1. **For starters, will he take this test:**

____ Eagerly?

____ Indifferently?

____ Kicking and screaming?

2. **Does he have his tonsils?**

____ Yes

____ No

3. **What does he generally do with junk mail?**

____ Throw it away without opening it

____ Skim it just in case

____ Read it carefully no matter what

4. **What's his boss's spouse's first name?**

5. **If you died tomorrow, how soon would he want to get into another relationship?**

____ Right away

____ In a while

____ Never

6. Which of these can't he do?

___ Make a decent cheese omelet

___ Do "walk the dog" with a yo-yo

___ Juggle three oranges

___ Sing the national anthem without missing a word

7. If you say "Cross your legs," will he:

___ Cross them at the ankles?

___ Cross them at the knees?

___ Put one ankle on the other knee?

8. Can you name at least one of his old flames—first and last name?

9. What's his shoe size?

10. How does he put on shoes and socks?

___ A sock and a sock, then a shoe and a shoe

___ A sock and a shoe, then a sock and a shoe

11. When was the last time he spoke—on the phone or in person—with one of his relatives? Which one?

12. Does he think he's more generous with:

____ Time? ____ Money?

13. Within four pounds, how much does he weigh?

14. Would he like to go to space?

____ He'd love it! ____ Are you kidding?

15. How many pairs of gloves or mittens does he own?

____ None ____ Two

____ One ____ Three or more

16. Does he kick left-footed or right-footed?

17. In which pocket does he usually carry his wallet?

18. And how many photos does he keep in it?

19. Where was his father born?

20. What's his mother's phone number?

21. If someone brought him to a casino and gave him a pile of chips, where would he take them?

_____ To a card game

_____ To the roulette table

_____ To the craps table

_____ To the cashier, to turn them in for money

22. Assuming he liked the location, would he rather have:

_____ A one-week vacation at a luxury hotel?

_____ A two-week vacation at a just-decent hotel?

23. What article of clothing did he buy for himself most recently?

24. Which of these classic films has he seen?

_____ *Gone with the Wind*

_____ *Star Wars: Episode IV – A New Hope*

_____ *Casablanca*

_____ *Frankenstein*

25. Does he believe in an afterlife?

_____ Definitely

_____ Definitely not

_____ He's uncertain

26. Which one of your friends does he find most attractive?

27. In a dentist's waiting room, which would he pick up?

_____ A health magazine

_____ A fashion magazine

_____ A news magazine

_____ A sports magazine

_____ None; he'd rather stare at the wall

28. If his fairy godmother offered him any car in the world, which would he choose? (Two bonus points if you know the color too.)

29. Did he have any pets as a child?

_____ Yes, a _____ named _____.

_____ No

30. Which parts of the newspaper, print or online, does he read regularly?

_____ Front page

_____ Sports

_____ Business

_____ Comics

_____ Obituaries

_____ Other

_____ He doesn't often read a newspaper

31. On vacation in an area he's never been to before, which would he head to first?

_____ A museum

_____ A historic site

_____ A sports arena

_____ Someplace else: _____

32. Can he raise one eyebrow at a time?

_____ Yes   _____ No

33. He's walking downtown. He glances at the sidewalk and discovers a wad of paper money. What does he do?

_____ Pocket it

_____ Look around for a store where he can buy himself something

_____ Start thinking about a gift for someone else

_____ Call the police to ask if someone reported lost money

34. Who did he vote for in the last big election?

35. Does he consider shopping for birthday, anniversary, or holiday cards:

_____ A pleasure?

_____ Pure drudgery (but he does it)?

_____ Something for you to do?

36. You're in an intimate French restaurant for dinner. The menu offers only two choices for each course. Which does he pick?

_____ Pâté	or	_____ Fresh melon
_____ Onion soup	or	_____ Vichyssoise
_____ Duck in orange sauce	or	_____ Steak in pepper sauce
_____ Chocolate mousse	or	_____ Lemon soufflé

37. What's his dress shirt size?

_____ Neck _____ Sleeve

38. What's his belt size?

39. Who cuts his hair? (If he has no hair, smile and take your ten points for free.)

40. Did he collect anything as a child?

_____ Yes, he collected _____.

_____ No

41. Can you name at least three of his childhood neighbors?

42. How many times a day does he brush his teeth?

_____ Zero

_____ One

_____ Two

_____ Three or more

43. What does he consider his best physical feature?

His _____.

44. Does he look at men's magazines that feature nudes?

_____ Often

_____ Sometimes

_____ Never

45. Does he think smoking marijuana should be legal?

___ Yes   ___ No

___ He's undecided

46. Name his elementary school.

47. Name the person he considers his closest friend.

48. How does he usually sign his name?

___ With his full legal name

___ With part left out

___ With one or more initials

___ With a nickname

49. Does he remember where you went on your first date together?

___ Yes   ___ No

50. If he won a huge lottery prize, what would he do?

_____ Quit work

_____ Take time off, but intend to return

_____ Keep working

51. Which household chore does he dislike most?

52. If you gave him some money and asked him to pick up something at the cleaners for you, what would he do with the change?

_____ Keep it   _____ Give it to you

53. You and he have just been presented with the bill for dinner at a restaurant. Because the waiter forgot to write down your appetizers, you have been undercharged. What does he do?

_____ Tell the waiter

_____ Say nothing and pay the bill

_____ Say nothing and leave a bigger tip, figuring the waiter undercharged you "as a favor"

54. Has he ever shot with a bow and arrow?

_____ Yes   _____ No

55. On a sweltering summer day, you stop for ice cream. Only four flavors are available. Does he pick:

____ Vanilla? ____ Strawberry?

____ Chocolate? ____ Pistachio?

56. How did he learn to drive a car?

57. Which is closest to his idea of a fun evening?

____ Watching TV or reading

____ Hanging out with friends or family

____ Going to a show or concert

58. What was his first job? (Even a part-time job he held as a youngster.)

59. Among your relatives, who's his favorite?

60. And his least favorite?

61. In which of the following would he like a free lesson from an expert? (Check as many as you think he'd choose.)

____ Cooking	____ Mixing drinks
____ Tennis	____ Cabinetmaking
____ Scuba diving	____ Fly-fishing
____ Auto repair	____ Needlepoint

62. What was his GPA in high school?

63. Given four ways to spend time in front of a screen, which of these would he choose?

____ A football game

____ A science or technology show

____ An episode of a fantasy drama series

____ An old movie

____ None

64. Has he read a book in the past year? Ten points if you know, and if he did, five bonus points if you can name it.

_____ Yes: _____.

_____ No

65. You're at a small gathering at a mutual friend's house. After some boring vacation videos, the friend starts to show very X-rated footage. What does your husband do?

_____ Leave the room

_____ Protest loudly

_____ Stay, with discomfort

_____ Stay, but tell you to leave

_____ Stay, and have a great time

66. And what would he do if you weren't there?

67. What would he say is the most common cause of arguments between you?

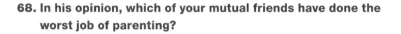

68. In his opinion, which of your mutual friends have done the worst job of parenting?

69. Does he ever walk around the house naked when no one else is there?

_____ Yes   _____ No

70. Does he think he keeps a secret well? (Forget what you think. What'll he say?)

_____ Yes   _____ No

71. Which habit of yours most annoys him?

72. How does he feel about his middle name? (Or, if he doesn't have one, how does he feel about not having one?)

_____ Likes it

_____ Hates it

_____ He's neutral

73. Who will he say is the funniest person he knows?

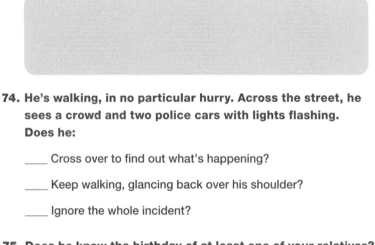

74. He's walking, in no particular hurry. Across the street, he sees a crowd and two police cars with lights flashing. Does he:

_____ Cross over to find out what's happening?

_____ Keep walking, glancing back over his shoulder?

_____ Ignore the whole incident?

75. Does he know the birthday of at least one of your relatives?

_____ Yes   _____ No

76. Has he ever had stitches? In what part of the body?

_____ Yes: _____.

_____ No

77. Does he drink plain water during the workday?

_____ A lot

_____ Now and then

_____ Never

78. Is he superstitious? Which of these does he fear, even a little?

____ Friday the 13th   ____ Spilled salt

____ Black cats   ____ Open umbrellas indoors

____ Broken mirrors   ____ None of these

79. He pulls into a metered parking space. There are eight minutes remaining on the meter. He's planning a ten-minute errand. What does he do?

____ Put in no money and not worry about it

____ Put in no money and try to rush through the errand

____ Put in a coin to be safe

80. When was the last time he wrote a non-work letter, email, or text to anyone?

____ No more than a few days ago

____ About a week or so ago

____ A month ago, at least

____ A year or more ago

81. Which statement best expresses his point of view about whether the mothers of young children should take a paying job?

____ "They should work outside the home if they like."

____ "They shouldn't unless the money is really needed."

82. What style funeral would he want?

_____ Large, formal

_____ Small, informal

_____ None

83. Does he have anything stashed away that was given to him—by you or anyone else—that he really can't stand?

_____ Yes, a _____.

_____ No

84. What's his favorite season?

_____ Spring   _____ Fall

_____ Summer   _____ Winter

85. "I could be reasonably happy earning twenty-five percent less than I earn now." Will he agree or disagree?

_____ Agree   _____ Disagree

86. Among your regular acquaintances, which couple would he least like to spend a long weekend with?

87. What does he think about the possibility of intelligent life on other planets?

_____ Very likely

_____ Possible, but not likely

_____ Out of the question

_____ He has no idea

88. Can he touch his elbows together behind his back?

_____ Yes   _____ No

89. With 1 being very calm and 5 being very high-strung, how nervous does he consider himself?

_____ 1

_____ 2

_____ 3

_____ 4

_____ 5

90. "Organized competitive sports are bad for kids because they overemphasize winning." What's his view?

_____ Agrees

_____ Disagrees

_____ Wouldn't give a simple yes or no

_____ No opinion

91. Since the age of eighteen, has he thrown liquid on a fully-clothed person?

____ Yes   ____ No

92. If he learned from a very reliable source that a close friend's partner was cheating, what would he do?

____ Tell the friend   ____ Confront the outsider

____ Write an anonymous note   ____ Ask for your advice

____ Confront the friend's partner   ____ Do nothing

93. How does he generally go to sleep?

____ On his back   ____ On his left side

____ On his stomach   ____ On his right side

94. If a serious fire broke out while he was at home, what object or objects would he try to save first, if any?

95. Does he ever pray by himself?

____ Yes   ____ No

96. Does he know his zodiac sign?

____ Yes   ____ No

97. He has looked up the meaning of a word in the past seven days—true or false?

_____ True   _____ False

98. How does he trim his toenails?

_____ With clippers   _____ With a file

_____ With scissors   _____ By picking at them

99. In how many languages can he count from one to five?

_____ One

_____ Two

_____ Three

_____ Four or more

100. Does he ever say "I love you" to anyone besides you?

_____ Yes, to _____.

_____ No

Copyright © 1989, 2004, 2020 by Carlinsky & Carlinsky, Inc.
Cover and internal design © 2020 by Sourcebooks
Cover design by Kerri Resnick

This publication is designed to provide accurate and authoritative information in regard to the subject matter covered. It is sold with the understanding that the publisher is not engaged in rendering legal, accounting, or other professional service. If legal advice or other expert assistance is required, the services of a competent professional person should be sought. —*From a Declaration of Principles Jointly Adopted by a Committee of the American Bar Association and a Committee of Publishers and Associations*

All brand names and product names used in this book are trademarks, registered trademarks, or trade names of their respective holders. Sourcebooks is not associated with any product or vendor in this book.

Published by Sourcebooks
P.O. Box 4410, Naperville, Illinois 60567-4410
(630) 961-3900
sourcebooks.com

Library of Congress Cataloging-in-Publication data is on file with the publisher

Printed and bound in the United States of America.

DR 10 9 8 7 6 5 4 3 2 1